ACCOUNT BOOK

12 Column Ledger

Name: ______________________

Phone: ______________________

Book Nº: ______

Made in United States
Orlando, FL
08 September 2024

51279690R00061